The Damp Camp

By Cameron Macintosh

Bren and I went camping with Mum and Mama.

"It will be fun!" Mama said to me.

We set up camp
in the big red van.

I had a pump for my bed.

Mama got a lamp.

Mum lit some big logs.

We had a snack.

When the sun set,
the camp got **so** wet!

And when we got up,
the camp was still very damp.

"Let's go home!" said Bren.

"Do not be a grump!"
said Mum.
"It will not be this wet
all day."

"Let's jump in the mud!"
said Mama.

"Look at Mama stomp
in the thick mud!" Bren said.

When we got back to camp, we got the stuff back in the van.

We were wet!

Jumping in mud was fun,
but we were glad
to get home!

CHECKING FOR MEANING

1. Where did the family set up camp? *(Literal)*

2. Why did the camp get wet? *(Literal)*

3. Why do you think everyone was glad to be home? *(Inferential)*

EXTENDING VOCABULARY

pump	What is a *pump*? Where else can you use a pump?
grump	What is a *grump*? How do you behave if you are grumpy?
stomp	Look at the word *stomp*. How many sounds do you hear? What other words have a similar meaning? E.g. stamp, tramp, plod.

MOVING BEYOND THE TEXT

1. Look at the picture on page 3 of the girl using the pump. Explain how she is pumping up her bed.

2. What events other than camping could be spoiled by rain? What happens at these events when it starts to rain?

3. Have you ever played in mud? Where were you? What did you do? Was it fun?

4. Do you enjoy camping? What do you like most about it? Is there anything you don't like? Why?

SPEED SOUNDS

| ft | mp | nd | nk | st |

PRACTICE WORDS

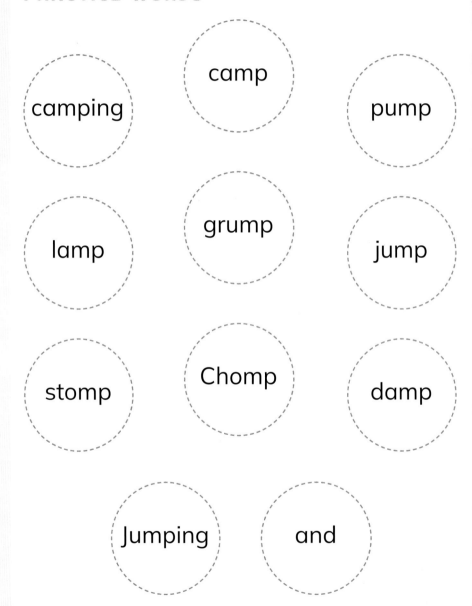

camping

camp

pump

lamp

grump

jump

stomp

Chomp

damp

Jumping

and